LOTTIE TOMLINSON'S

RAINBOW ROOTS

LAURENCE KING

Published in 2017 by Laurence King
Publishing Ltd
361–373 City Road
London EC1V 1LR
United Kingdom
Tel: +44 (0)20 7841 6900
Fax: +44 (0)20 7841 6910
e-mail: enquiries@laurenceking.com
www.laurenceking.com

A catalogue record for this book is
available from the British Library

ISBN: 978-1-78627-062-7

Edited and compiled by Natalie Theo
Design by The Digital Fairy
Photography by Olivia Richardson
Selfies by Lottie Tomlinson
Shoot production and additional
photography by The Book Agency
Sticker illustrations by Gabriella Sanchez
Cover photography by Hugo Yangüela

Printed in China

LOTTIE TOMLINSON'S

RAINBOW ROOTS

#MAKEUPBYME

Lottie Tomlinson
Edited and compiled by Natalie Theo

For my mum ... who was my biggest fan and always believed in me.

Everything I do is for her – my biggest inspiration.

I love and miss you every day.

X

RED
24

PINK
50

GREEN
70

PURPLE
80

ORANGE
94

BLUE
104

FOREWORD

BY LOU TEASDALE

A couple of years into my four-year tour with One Direction, as their hair and makeup artist, Louis's mum rang me out of the blue to spring it on me that, due to some disappointing GSCE results, I would be acquiring a new assistant in his younger sister Lottie. 'Of course, that's absolutely fine with me,' I assured Jay. I would take her eldest daughter under my wing and show her the ropes. I thought at the time, she won't actually get anywhere, in any way, but it's 'totally cool!', whilst also thinking to myself that this sounded like one massive babysitting job, which is the last thing you want on tour. But, nonetheless, I'd met Lottie before and she was cute, so hey ho. The NEXT DAY she was on a flight and, before I knew it, I was suddenly one half of everyone's favourite glam duo.

Two months and an appraisal in, I'd realised my babysitting role was quite the opposite. I NEEDED this girl and didn't want her to leave ... ever! I'd had some good assistants in the past (and some bad ones) but this was heaven –

she cleaned all the shit, she set up and cleared up without me even noticing. She picked all the little bits out of the main kit that I like to use in my personal makeup bag, and put them in my handbag every night with a diet coke, some chocolate and my phone charger, on my seat, ready and waiting in the car for me to run off stage carefree. It's the little things, eh :)

I mean, let's face it, she wasn't getting sent home was she? She was in a privileged position and she didn't really need to 'work hard' to keep it. However, she did. And I have the utmost respect for anyone with drive and a good work ethic. Unfortunately for me, said ethic, combined with the potential of this budding beauty influencer with 3 million followers, has left me with no assistant. I am proud to support her flourishing in her own right and to introduce her to you, with her first publication – *Rainbow Roots*, by my best friend, Lottie Tomlinson.

HOW I FOUND MY RAINBOW ROOTS

It all started when I was about 12. I used to spend hours on the Benefit and MAC websites, memorising all their products. They were my two favourites! One day my mum said that I could order one thing, so I chose the Benefit Erase Paste and from that one product I began to build my collection.

I was lucky enough to grow up with sisters, so I practised on them and on myself, constantly experimenting. It didn't take long for me to realise that there are no rules when it comes to makeup. When you're in your room doing nothing ... experiment! Discover what you love. Makeup is not permanent. It wipes off. Do it. Wipe it off. If it goes wrong just try again. That's part of the fun.

My professional career started at 16, once I'd finished my GCSEs. Unfortunately, even though I really wanted to, I didn't get the grades to stay on at school, but I didn't let that stand in my way.

I soon started working with Lou Teasdale who was on tour with One Direction. I asked if I could assist her with anything, literally anything, so that I could learn, and that's when I picked up most of my skills. I just carried on and never really went home. I was so happy!

I found my true rainbow roots and followed my passion. Now I get to do what I love every day.

Remember:

- Be yourself
- There are NO rules
- Don't follow trends or seasons
- Don't take yourself too seriously
- Do whatever you want for rainbows every day!

THE BASICS

TOOLS OF THE TRADE

GET STARTED WITH MY KIT HIT LIST.

For work I travel with a HUGE suitcase, and I have entire kit bags devoted to skin, lips, eyes, palettes and brushes. But for myself I have two small black makeup bags that I take everywhere with me.

But, you don't even need that! A few key essentials will get you started.

Build up your kit slowly, starting with the basics. These are the things I couldn't live without:

BROW GEL
Brows frame your face. Always use something like a brow gel to set them.

POWDER
To sort out the shine.

CONCEALER
It's more important to have a concealer than a foundation. Plus, it's easy to adapt a concealer to be your foundation if you don't need a lot.

MASCARA
A must.

LIP BALM
Even if you're not wearing lipstick you'll look quite done with a bit of balm.

HAVE A LOOK AT THE GLOSSARY (P.118) TO FIND OUT MORE ABOUT THE KEY PRODUCTS I USE IN THIS BOOK.

BRONZER
I always like to look bronzed!

A LITTLE STUMPY BRUSH
For tidying up eyes, concealer ... anything.

BEAUTY BLENDER
This is one of my essentials because you can use it for everything from foundation, to bronzer to powder. It's sick.

A FLUFFY BRUSH
For blending around the eyes.

A DENSE BRUSH
For applying powders, eyeshadows, creams ... and glitter. It really picks up and applies a lot of pigment.

FACE ON

APPLY, BLEND, CONTOUR, SET FOR FLAWLESS SKIN.

APPLY THE BASE.

01 Pump a bit of foundation onto the back of your hand.

02 Dot it over the face with your finger, dabbing more on areas that need it. I like to use my fingers so I have more control.

03 Blend with a kabuki brush.

BLEND THE HIGH POINTS.

TO USE A BEAUTY BLENDER, WET IT AND SQUEEZE OUT THE EXCESS. THIS MAKES IT BIGGER, BOUNCIER AND BETTER FOR BLENDING.

01 Dot concealer under your eyes and on your nose and chin.

02 Blend with a beauty blender to get more coverage. Cover any blemishes and blend again to finish.

CONTOUR *LIKE A PRO TO MAKE YOUR FEATURES POP.*

01 Apply contouring colour under cheekbone and upper hair line.

02 Blend using a kabuki brush for a seamless finish.

WHEN PICKING FOUNDATION SHADES, MATCH THE FOUNDATION TO YOUR NECK RATHER THAN YOUR FACE. THAT'S WHERE YOU WANT THE COLOUR TO MATCH BEST.

SET WITH TRANSLUCENT POWDER. YOU'RE PACKING A LOT ON, SO TRANSLUCENT POWDER WILL STOP IT GETTING CAKEY.

01 Pack on the powder with a beauty blender, just under the eyes, and leave to set for a few minutes.

02 Once set, knock off any excess powder with a big fluffy brush.

03 Use a powder compact foundation that is creamier to set the rest of your face. I use a kabuki brush.

THIS TECHNIQUE IS CALLED 'BAKING.' I HEARD IT ORIGINATED FROM DRAG QUEENS.

SELF-TAN

Get orange-a-tanned! I couldn't live without a tan.

Self-tan first timers, use a moisturiser with a gradual tan in it. These are foolproof. You'll get a natural, subtle colour.

If you mess up, jump in the shower and use a body scrub.

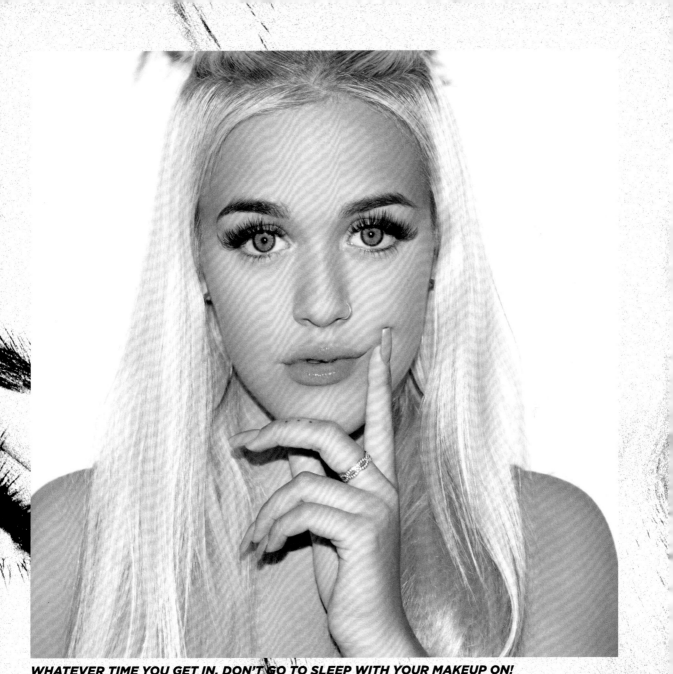

WHATEVER TIME YOU GET IN, DON'T GO TO SLEEP WITH YOUR MAKEUP ON! CLEANSE, TONE AND MOISTURISE ... ALWAYS!

BROWS

ALWAYS APPLY YOUR BROWS.

01 Comb through your brows with a brush-on brow gel so all the hairs go in the right direction.

02 Fill any gaps with a cream brow gel using an angled brush. Make them as thick or as thin as you want ...

03 Use an angled brush to apply concealer above the arch of the brow, and directly beneath, to accentuate the shape.

04 For more precision, tidy up with a fine pointy brush.

05 Then blend with a fluffy brush.

FOR THAT FINAL BIT OF DRAMA, ADD LASHES. THE BIGGER THE BETTER.

IF USING A BROW PENCIL, REMEMBER YOU'RE NOT COLOURING IN! TRY TO MAKE HAIR-LIKE STROKES TO CREATE A MORE NATURAL LOOK.

HAIRSPO

GIVE ANY LOOK THAT FINISHING TOUCH.

Look for inspiration everywhere. I've tried every colour of the rainbow when it comes to my hair, and Gwen Stefani was the inspiration for the first time I dyed my hair pink. Pink seems to go with everything and I always tend to go back to it!

I love getting my hair done at BLEACH. They are always up for trying something different. Just like me. When we created the rainbow roots hair, we were just freestyling with ideas. The result was sick.

THRILLS AND SPILLS
Inspired by Alex Brownsell's iconic *i-D* cover for The Just Kids Issue with FKA Twigs. We experimented with colour for a different take on rainbow roots.

SPACE BUNS
When I want to make a statement I go for space buns.

I WOULDN'T EVEN ATTEMPT TO BLEACH YOUR HAIR AT HOME, I THINK IT'S A DISASTER WAITING TO HAPPEN.

LOOSE WAVES
For clubbing ... I love going for loose waves using a big hair tong. Make sure to let the waves cool down so they set and then brush them out for a more natural look.

HIGH PONY
High ponies are great if you've gone all out with your makeup and you want the focus to be on your face.

MESSY BUN
My favourite hair for lazy days is definitely a messy bun! You can't beat chilling with your hair shoved up.

BRAIDS
Braids are perfect for festivals and cool holiday looks.

NOW YOU'RE READY. USE COLOUR TO EXPRESS YOURSELF. GET INSPIRED! CREATE YOUR OWN RAINBOW ROOTS.

RED
SIRENS

MATTE LIP

28

GLOSSY LIP

29

GLITTER LIP

30

OMBRE LIP

32

SEEING RED

36

GLOSSY LIDS

37

MATTE LIP

BRIGHT COLOURS LOOK GREAT IN MATTE. THIS IS A GOOD WAY TO TRY OUT A RED FOR THE FIRST TIME. IT'S LESS SCARY AND NOT SO IN-YOUR-FACE.

APPLY POWDER ON THE LIPS FIRST TO CREATE AN EVEN BASE.

I USE LIQUID LIPSTICK BECAUSE IT'S LONG-LASTING. REMEMBER IT DRIES FAST!

YOU DON'T NEED LIP LINER WHEN YOU'RE USING LIQUID LIPSTICK. JUST A STEADY HAND!

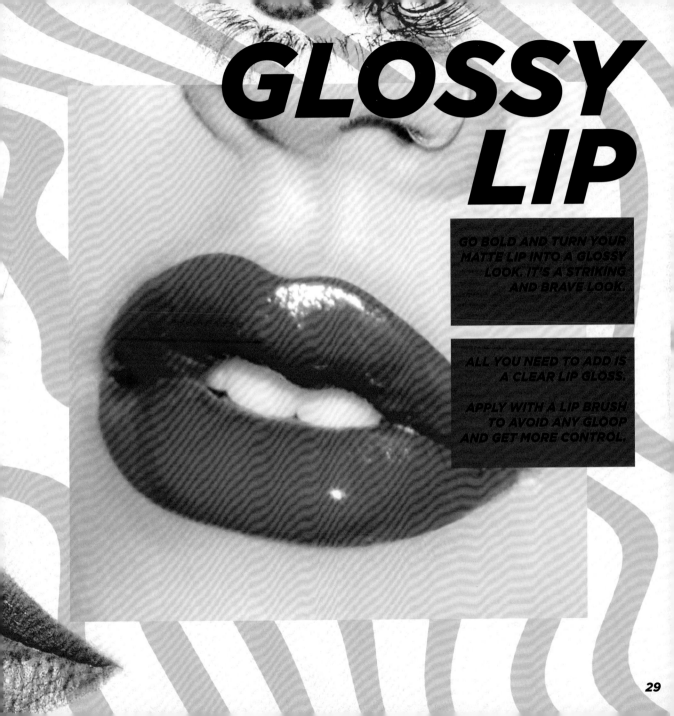

GLOSSY LIP

GO BOLD AND TURN YOUR MATTE LIP INTO A GLOSSY LOOK. IT'S A STRIKING AND BRAVE LOOK.

ALL YOU NEED TO ADD IS A CLEAR LIP GLOSS.

APPLY WITH A LIP BRUSH TO AVOID ANY GLOOP AND GET MORE CONTROL.

GLITTER LIP

DO THIS LOOK FOR A FESTIVAL OR RAVE TO STAND OUT FROM THE CROWD.

01 Start with your Glossy Lip (previous page).

02 Use a dense brush to pack on the glitter. If the brush is fluffy then the glitter will fall all over your face.

03 Fill in the corners of the mouth with a fine lip brush for a more precise finish.

MIX AND MASH UP YOUR LIP COLOURS. I'VE USED TWO SHADES OF RED HERE – A LIGHT AND A DARK.

01 Line and fill the outer lips with dark liner.

02 Dot the lighter shade onto the centre.

03 Blend with a blending brush. It's ok if you go over the darker lines as you can always fill them in again with the liner.

OMBRE LIP

TAKE A TREND AND WORK OUT
HOW YOU CAN MAKE IT DIFFERENT.

*TRY A TOTAL COLOUR CONTRAST,
OR ADD A THIRD SHADE (SEE P.99)*

DATE NIGHT READY

SEEING RED

EXPERIMENT WITH YOUR MAKEUP AND DO SOME DIY.

01 Apply a red lip liner to the waterline, and use a dense brush to add red pigmented gloss on the lower lash line. Blend.

02 Apply a wet colour or lip gloss to the bottom lashes. It's DIY red mascara.

DENSE BRUSHES ARE GOOD FOR BUFFING CREAM PRODUCTS INTO THE SKIN.

GLOSSY LIDS

YOU CAN DO THIS WITH ANY COLOUR, BUT RED REALLY POPS.

04 With a softer, fluffy brush get a little bit of blend going.

01 Apply a paint stick to your lids.

05 Finally, apply a red, or clear, lip gloss over the lids.

02 Pack on colour with a dense brush. Add more to the centres of the lids to build up the pigmentation.

03 Make a subtle wing shape and don't go too close to the lash line.

SELFIE
SUNSHINE

42

COLOUR
CLASH

44

UNDER-EYE
NEON FLICK

SELFIE SUNSHINE

THIS LOOK IS ABOUT COMBINING YELLOW CREAM WITH A POWDER ON TOP. THE PERFECT BLEND.

01 Apply a cream colour as a base at the centre of the lid, towards the inner eye. Don't cover the entire lid.

02 Apply the same base below the eye, from corner to corner.

03 Blend a yellow powder over the cream, above and below the eye.

COLOUR

BLEND THE HOTTEST SHADES AND EXPERIMENT WITH COLOUR CLASH.

01 Want your eyeshadow to stay on? Apply primer first. Don't forget the lower lash line.

02 Pack yellow over the centre of the lid with a dense brush.

03 Do the same on the lower lash line – just into the centre.

CLASH

04 Add your pop of pink above the yellow, along the crease.

05 Blend.

06 Apply more pink to the bottom outer corner, under the lash line, and blend.

DON'T HOLD BACK ON COLOUR. GO FOR HIGH-VISIBILITY CONTRASTS.

45

RAVE LOOKS

UNDER-EYE NEON FLICK

NEVER HOLD BACK WITH NEON – IT CAN BE USED FOR ANYTHING.

01 ☺

02 ☺

01 Use an angled eyeliner brush to add a line to the lower lash line, exaggerating the flicks. Don't worry about getting yellow in your lashes!

02 Keep checking in the mirror and balance out those flicks.

USE DOTS AS A MAKESHIFT

STENCIL TO GET THE

PERFECT FLICK.

TURN IT UP Use an orange eyeliner pot to apply colour to your waterline with a flat-winged eyeliner brush.

49

THINK
PINK

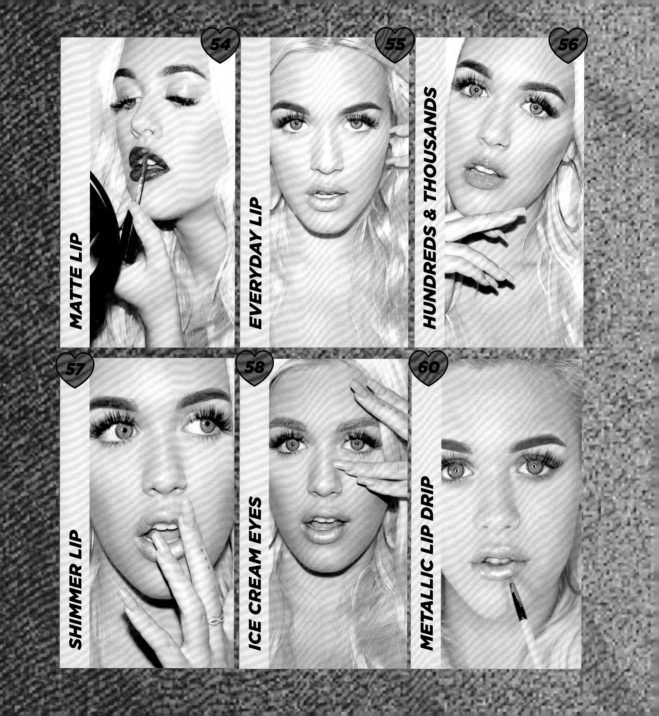

54 MATTE LIP

55 EVERYDAY LIP

56 HUNDREDS & THOUSANDS

57 SHIMMER LIP

58 ICE CREAM EYES

60 METALLIC LIP DRIP

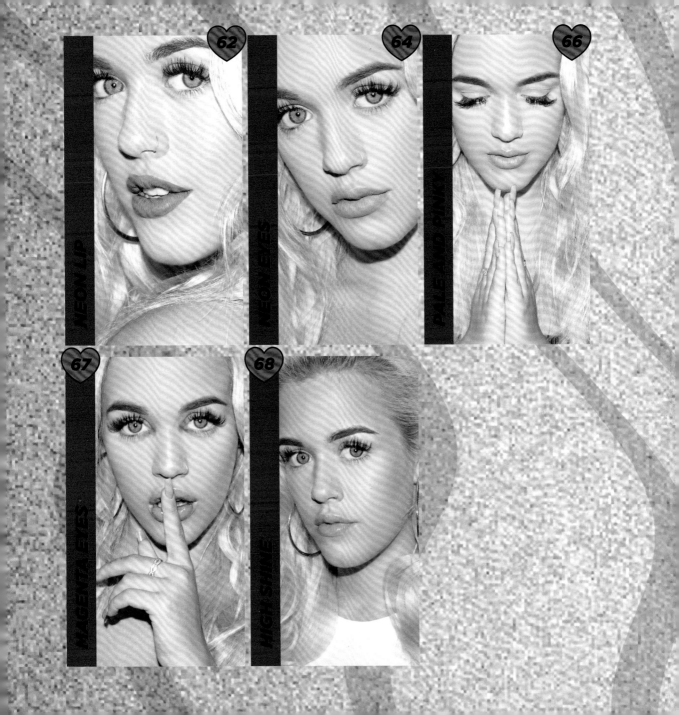

MATTE LIP

BRIGHT LOOKS BETTER MATTE.

01 Powder lips.

02 Line lips with a nude pencil lip liner.

03 Mark a line down the centre of the bottom lip with the pencil. Lips will look fuller. Light colours will pop.

04 Finish with a softer shade of shimmery lip gloss.

EVERYDAY LIP

EVERYDAY LIP PERFECTION.

HUNDREDS & THOUSANDS

GET CREATIVE. MIX GLITTER AND GLOSS TO MAKE YOUR OWN HUNDREDS & THOUSANDS LOOK.

01 Dab lips with a soft pink colour.

02 Add sprinkles of glitter to a clear lip gloss. Mix it all up.

03 Coat lips in your new gloss using a lip brush.

SHIMMER LIP

01 Apply a pink lipstick.

02 Press pink shimmer powder onto your lips with a flat shading brush.

03 Pat more colour on with your fingers to intensify.

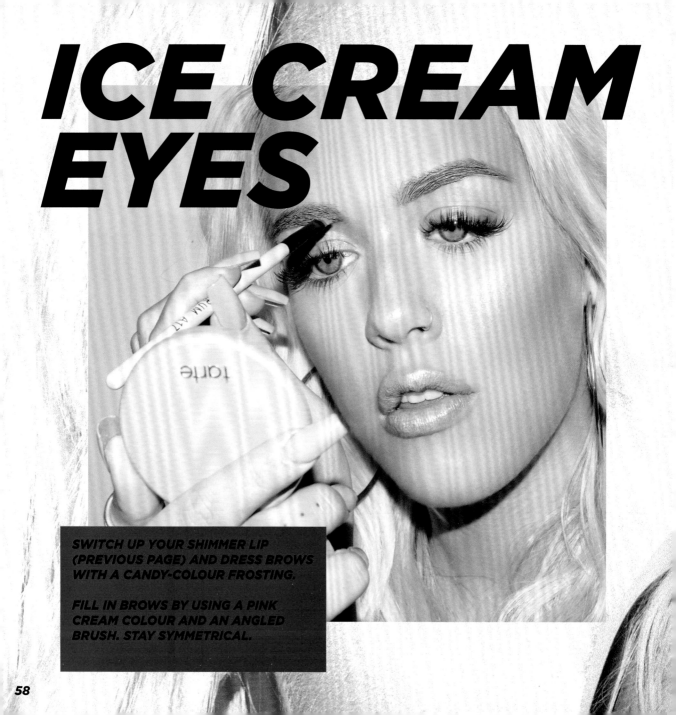

ICE CREAM EYES

SWITCH UP YOUR SHIMMER LIP (PREVIOUS PAGE) AND DRESS BROWS WITH A CANDY-COLOUR FROSTING.

FILL IN BROWS BY USING A PINK CREAM COLOUR AND AN ANGLED BRUSH. STAY SYMMETRICAL.

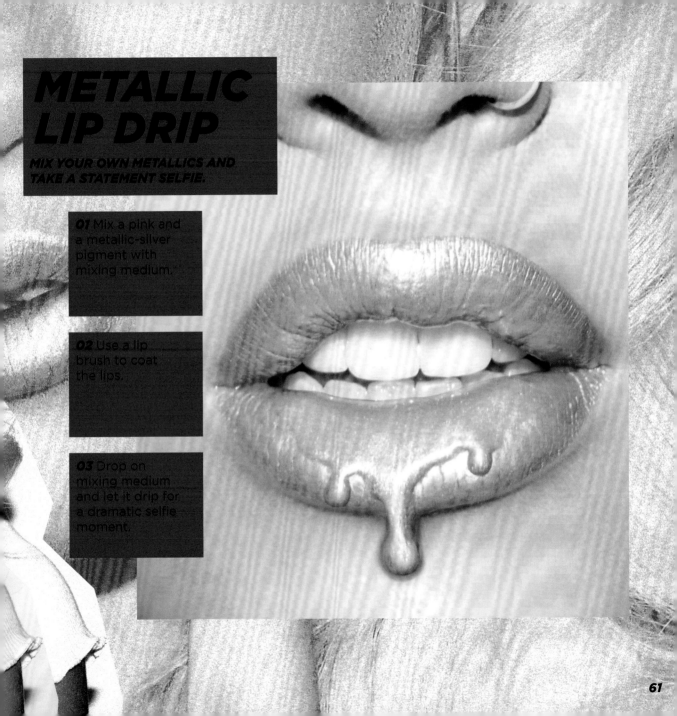

METALLIC LIP DRIP

MIX YOUR OWN METALLICS AND TAKE A STATEMENT SELFIE.

01 Mix a pink and a metallic-silver pigment with mixing medium.

02 Use a lip brush to coat the lips.

03 Drop on mixing medium and let it drip for a dramatic selfie moment.

NEONS ARE SICK! I LOVE THEM BECAUSE THEY'RE SO BRIGHT AND STAND OUT. THEY CAN MAKE ANYTHING LOOK COOL.

01 Blend a little bronzer onto your lids for a neutral look.

02 Add mascara.

03 Go neon pink on the lips with liquid lipstick.

04 Pat to even out the texture then leave to dry.

NEON LIP

FLAWLESS SKIN AND MINIMAL EYES MAKE NEON LIPS THE STARS

NEON
EYES

**EYES GO FLUORO,
LIPS GO LOW-KEY.**

01 Apply nude concealer to your eyelid for a clean base.

02 Create a bold waterline with a neon pink.

03 Powder the lips with foundation for a clean base.

04 Add a pale nude lip and lip gloss to finish.

PALE AND PINKY

MULTI-TASK CREAMS FOR EYES, CHEEKS OR LIPS.

01

02

IF YOU WANT, PACK A DUSTING OF TRANSLUCENT POWDER ON TOP TO STAY TIDY. I LIKE IT WITHOUT. A LITTLE MESS IS GOOD!

01 Apply colour to the lids.

02 Line the crease of the eye with a flat-angled brush and fill.

03 Keep checking that the colour stays within the crease.

04 Pack a dusting of translucent powder on top if you want it to stay tidy.

05 Balance out with a nude lip gloss.

01 Apply eye primer to the corner of the eye to help the pigment stick.

02 Use a dense brush to pack the pigment onto the inner corners.

DIP YOUR BRUSH INTO THE PIGMENT AND TAP IT BEFORE YOU APPLY.

03 Blend – just a little. Keep it piled on.

04 Add a pale nude lip.

USE PIGMENTS FOR PUNCHY EYES. DON'T KILL ANY SPILL: SNAP AND POST.

01 Apply a creamy highlighter with fingers just above the cheekbones.

02 Blend with a beauty blender.

03 Use a fan brush to add a highlighter powder.

04 Blend.

68

HIGH SHINE

LET YOUR SKIN CATCH THE LIGHT WITH A CREAM-BASED HIGHLIGHTER.

MERMAID
LIP

SEA PUNK
EYES

76

MERMAID LIP

FIND YOUR FAVOURITE SALTY SHADE AND LAYER IT UP.

USE OIL-BASED BEAUTY CLEANSERS TO STRIP COLOURS.

SEA PUNK EYES

GIVE YOUR INNER MERMAID A BIT OF EDGE.

01 Create a base by brushing a dark purple lipstick onto your eyelids and blend with a fluffy brush.

02 Apply a green pigment to the centre of the lid with a dense brush. Blend.

03 Smudge the green under the eye and into the waterline with a short, stumpy brush.

TOUGHEN UP LOOKS. PLAY WITH RAINBOW COLOURS.

PRISMATIC

GOTH
LIP

84

RIHANNA
LIP

86

88

DISCO GLITTER LIDS

92

PURPLE HAZE

GOTH LIP

PAIR A DRAMATIC COLOUR WITH A BLACK EYELINER.

LINE YOUR LIPS WITH A BLACK EYELINER. A LINER STOPS THE COLOUR FROM BLEEDING OUT. FILL WITH ANY COLOUR FOR THAT GOTH EFFECT.

RIHANNA LIP

RIHANNA IS THE ULTIMATE INSPO AND SHE ALWAYS ROCKS A STATEMENT LIP.

01 Use a lip scrub to exfoliate. It makes lips nice and smooth, ready for any lip colour.

02 Apply lip balm.

03 Powder lips to make them matte. Now you're prepped and ready for colour.

04 Apply liquid lipstick with a lip brush for perfect precision.

IT'S ALWAYS GOOD TO PREP YOUR LIPS WHEN USING A LIQUID LIPSTICK.

USE FINE GLITTER FOR A MORE NATURAL LOOK AND CHUNKY GLITTER FOR MORE DRAMA.

01 Apply a white base up to the eye crease, then blend.

02 Add purple eyeshadow with a flat shading brush. Blend again.

03 Brush a mixing medium over the colour with a dense brush.

04 Pack on as much glitter as possible with the dense brush.

A FLUFFY BRUSH WILL TIDY UP ANY GLITTER SPILL.

DISCO GLITTER LIDS

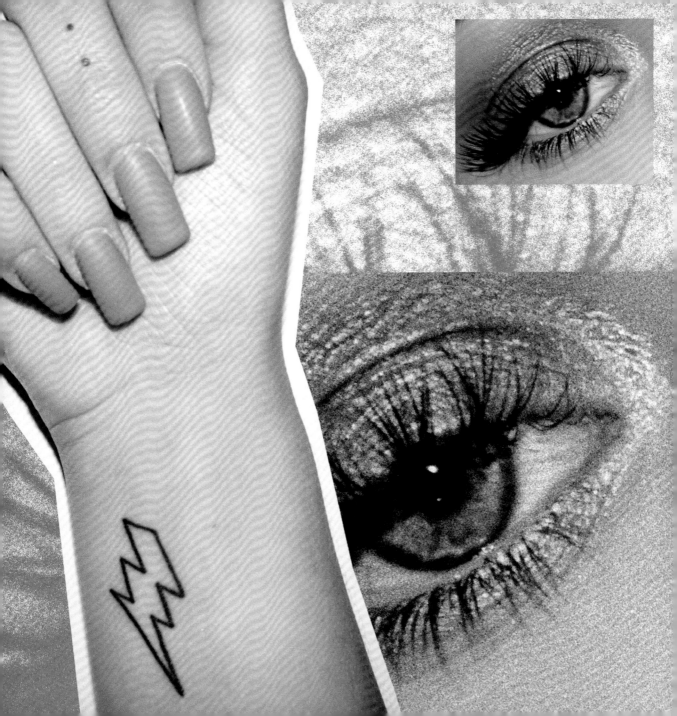

PURPLE HAZE

TRY AN ALTERNATIVE TO A BLACK SMOKY EYE.

01 Blend a dark purple into the inner and outer corner of the lid. Blend into the crease to soften lines and avoid making a mess.

02 Add a shimmery purple shade to the centre of the lid for a pop of colour. Use a flat shading brush.

03 Repeat on the lower lash line using a pencil brush.

04 Add black to the waterline.

ORANGE
BITES

98

FIRE
LIPS

99

SEEING DOUBLE
100

SUBTLE
SMOKE
102

ORANGE BITES

**BE BOLD.
LAYER ON
THE LIPSTICK.**

**IF YOU WANT A
MATTE LIP BUT DON'T
HAVE THE RIGHT
LIPSTICK, YOU CAN
APPLY TRANSLUCENT
POWDER OVER THE
TOP TO CREATE A DIY
MATTE LIQUID LIP.**

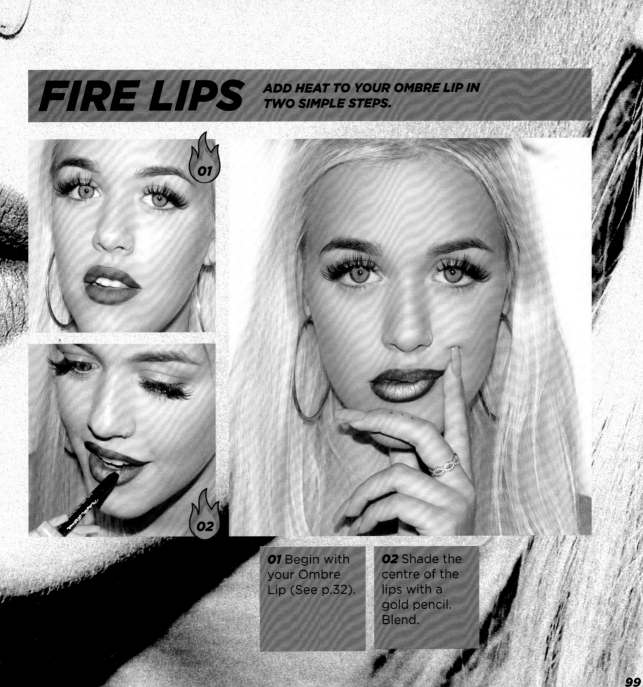

FIRE LIPS

ADD HEAT TO YOUR OMBRE LIP IN TWO SIMPLE STEPS.

01 Begin with your Ombre Lip (See p.32).

02 Shade the centre of the lips with a gold pencil. Blend.

SEEING
DOUBLE
DOUBLE
SEEING

PLAY A BALANCING ACT WITH THIS HOT PUNCHY SHADE.

01 Use a liquid lipstick wand to apply smudgy dots under your lashes.

02 Check the mirror. Make sure they are centered.

03 Use the same liquid lipstick for your lips.

SUBTLE SMOKE

COMBINE CREAM AND POWDER IN SHADES OF ORANGE FOR THIS SUBTLE TAKE ON AN EVENING LOOK.

01 Use a fluffy brush to cover lids with a bright orange cream colour.

02 Add a darker, brick-orange powder on top.

03 Apply this shade under the lower lash line. Blend.

BLUE DENIM
DAYS

BIRO
LIP

109

FESTIVAL EYES

112

BLUE SEQUIN EYES

114

BIRO LIP

TAKE A TREND AND REVERSE IT. THIS IS A NEW TAKE ON THE OMBRE LIP.

LEAVE THE OUTSIDE OF THE LIPS BARE, AND DOT THE BLUE LIP COLOUR ONTO THE CENTRE OF YOUR LIPS. BLEND.

BLUE DENIM DAYS

WEAR DENIM FOR DAYS, AND NOT JUST WITH YOUR JEANS.

01

02

01 Apply a white highlight powder to the inner corners. This will make the blue pop.

02 Cover your lids in a dark blue shade and blend out.

01 Apply a light blue shadow to the lids and blend.

02 Apply and blend on lower lash line.

03 Use a mixing medium to make jewels stick. I used a lip balm.

04 Wet the end of a makeup brush to pick up jewels and apply.

FESTIVAL EYES

EXPERIMENT WITH SHAPE AND PATTERN.

BLUE SEQUIN EYES

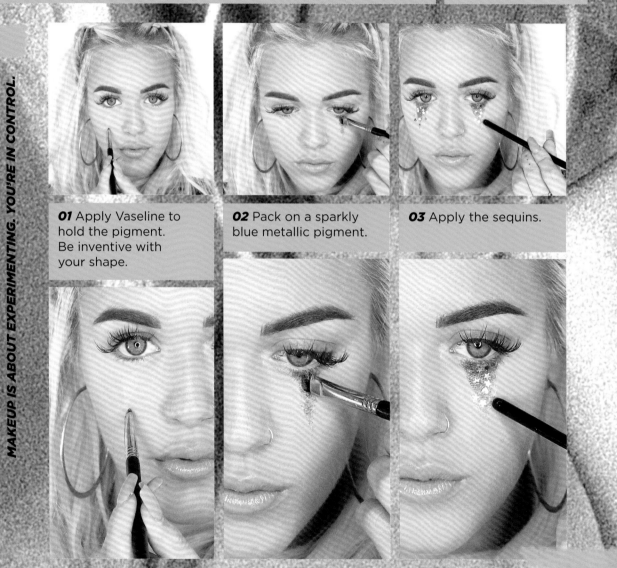

MAKEUP IS ABOUT EXPERIMENTING. YOU'RE IN CONTROL.

01 Apply Vaseline to hold the pigment. Be inventive with your shape.

02 Pack on a sparkly blue metallic pigment.

03 Apply the sequins.

114

GLOSSary

BRUSHES

Some brushes do a better job of blending, others do a great job of applying. But they can double up if you want them to.

ANGLED BRUSH

A brush with an angled head. Used for creating precise brows. Just what you need to create perfect lines when applying eyeliner, gel to brows or when creating an eye flick.

BEAUTY BLENDER

This is one of my essentials. It's a pear-shaped sponge and can be used for both applying and blending everything from foundations and concealers, to blushers and powders.

FLUFFY BRUSHES

Use a fluffy brush to blend. I use a small fluffy brush to blend out eye colours and tidy up any glitter spill. Fluffy brushes are also good for applying bronzer, blusher and highlighters. Sometimes I use this to apply lipstick to my eyelids, too. Like I said, there are no rules.

DENSE BRUSH

Use a dense brush to apply. They are good for really packing colour onto the eyes, and great for applying coloured pigments, shadows and creams to the eye … and, of course, glitter!

BLUSHER BRUSH

Effectively a big, fluffy blending brush. Use for blending powder or cream blushes onto cheeks.

STUMPY BRUSHES

Another type of dense brush for the eyes. This brush is perfect for applying and/or smudging product under the eye.

FINE POINTY BRUSH

This has a small fine head, perfect for filling in brows, creating a perfect pout and anytime you want really precise, sharp lines.

FAN BRUSH

Shaped like a fan – obviously – this little number is perfect for applying highlighter.

PENCIL BRUSH

The end of this brush tapers like a pencil, making it perfect for smudging or shading along the eye line.

KABUKI BRUSH

This gives me that flawless finish when buffing foundation powders into skin.

FLAT SHADING BRUSH

A dense brush that you can use to build up shadow on the eye, and to blend for a dense colour.

WINGED EYELINER BRUSH

Shaped like a wing and used to create a winged eye.

LIP BRUSH

This is a flat brush used to apply lipstick, or paint sticks, to lips.

MAKEUP

I love multi-tasking products and the colours I use do just that. This means you can get creative, be inventive and really experiment with your looks.

BROW GEL

A coloured gel formula used for filling in and defining eyebrows.

CREAM COLOUR

Use these for anything from lids, to eye lines, to lips. They're great as a coloured base on the eye, especially when you want to build up really punchy tones. Apply coloured eyeshadows on top, or just add gloss for a glossy lid.

EYELINER POT

Eyeliner in the form of a gel. Apart from being used to line the lash line, these can be used on the lids as a coloured base.

LIQUID LIPSTICK

A long-lasting liquid version of lipstick. These colours are really pigmented and punchy and great for making bold lip statements. Once applied they dry quickly!

MIXING MEDIUM

This is a colourless liquid that lets you create your own unique product when mixed with pigments.

PAINT STICK

Multi-tasking cream colour in the form of a stick. Great for eyes and lips and my Glossy Lids (see p.37).

PIGMENTS

Pigments are loose eyeshadow powders that are either neon or metallic. They are not just for the eyes! They work well with a mixing medium to create your own wicked lip colours.

POWDER COLOUR

Coloured eye powders or eyeshadows are great layered over cream colours, or just worn on their own.

SHIMMER POWDER

A powder that has a glittery shimmer effect to it: think powdery metallic. They're usually sold as eyeshadows but can be used on lips, cheeks or as highlighter.

TRANSLUSCENT POWDER

This is a matte powder that has no colour. I dust it over my makeup to hold it in place.

WHITE HIGHLIGHT POWDER

Makes the eyes pop when applied to the inner corners.

SKINCARE

LIP SCRUB

This is an exfoliator for lips. It's great for prepping, especially before using liquid lipstick, and ensures a really smooth finish.

OIL-BASED BEAUTY CLEANSER

The best makeup remover, especially for long-lasting liquid lipstick. The oil base lifts the product off the skin with ease.

NAILS

ACRYLICS

Acrylics are made of a mix of powder and liquid. They are usually clear, and you apply your colour after. I love acrylics because I can have whatever shape I want.

GEL NAILS

Gel nails are applied like a nail varnish with a base coat, colour and top coat. They're dried and set under UV lights.

DIRECTORY

PEOPLE

ALEX BROWNSELL @alexbrownsell
LOU TEASDALE @louteasdale
BEAUTY MEETS VIDEO @beautymeetsvideo
ZARRA CELIK @zarraceliknails

PRODUCTS

ANASTASIA BEVERLY HILLS
@anastasiabeverlyhills
ARMANI BEAUTY @armanibeauty
BARRY M @barrymcosmetics
BENEFIT COSMETICS
@benefitcosmeticsuk/@benefitcosmeticsus
BOBBI BROWN @bobbibrown
CHARLOTTE TILBURY @ctilburymakeup
COLOURPOP @colourpopcosmetics
COVER | FX @coverfx
DIOR MAKEUP @diormakeup
ESTÉE LAUDER @esteelauder
GLITTER INJECTIONS @glitterinjections
HOURGLASS @hourglasscosmetics
HUDA KATTAN @hudabeauty
ICONIC LONDON @iconic.london
JOUER COSMETICS @jouercosmetics

KAT VON D @katvondbeauty
KYLIE COSMETICS @kyliecosmetics
LIME CRIME @limecrimemakeup
MAC COSMETICS @maccosmetics
MILK MAKEUP @milkmakeup
MAYBELLINE @maybelline
NAILS INC @nailsinc
NIP + FAB @nipandfab
NYX PROFESSIONAL MAKEUP
@nyxcosmetics
OBSESSIVE COMPULSIVE COSMETICS
@occmakeup
SPECTRUM COLLECTIONS
@spectrumcollections
TARTE COSMETICS @tartecosmetics
3INA @3ina
URBAN DECAY COSMETICS
@urbandecaycosmetics
ZOEVA @zoevacosmetics

PLACES

BLEACH LONDON @bleachlondon
MAV LASH EXTENSIONS
@mavlashextensions
TOPSHOP @topshop
TOTALLY FABULASH @totallyfabulash